The Sea in Me

Jeannie Lawson

The Sea in Me

Thanks

Thank you to the wonderful people who became readers for this book of poems – some friends, some poets, some strangers – John Blackhawk, Val Norris, John Nankivell, Jennifer Garner and Paul Rooms. Your insight has helped shape these pages.

This book is dedicated to the many people who have supported and indulged my love of writing poetry over the years, especially my husband, David, who openly admits he only understands the ones that rhyme.

It is also dedicated to all those who love nature.
Please immerse yourself in it as often as possible.

The Sea in Me
ISBN 978 1 76109 515 3
Copyright © text Jeannie Lawson 2023
Cover image: Lisa Skelton Photography,
taken on the author's first whale swim in Tonga, 2016

First published 2023 by
GINNINDERRA PRESS
PO Box 3461 Port Adelaide 5015
www.ginninderrapress.com.au

Contents

Sunday Worship	7
Myriad	8
Essence	9
Origin	11
Heart-trails	12
Lonely Chapel	13
February Lilies	14
A Walk in the Wetland	15
Soundless…	16
Gondwana	17
Sea Child	18
Vocation	19
Wreck Dive	21
The Loch Ard Peacock	22
Sea Spirits	24
Shearwater	25
ANZAC Storm 2015	26
Second-hand War	27
My Nightmare	29
Adrift	30
Sunset Song	31
The Time Box	33
Stars of Earth	34
Just Add Water	35
Interwoven	37
Immersed	38
Serenade	39
Sea	40
Hawkesbury	41
Wild Places	43

Top End	44
Beyond The Wall	45
Tea Towels	46
Bird Language	47
Strangest Fruit	48
No Trace	49
The Voice in the Sea	50
Extinction	52
Sorrow	53
Cycles	55
Becoming	56
Sacred Exchange	57
August Rising	58
Tanilba	60
Rainbow Refuge	61
Dispersal	62
Haiku	64
Quest	65
Earthed	66
About the Author	67

Sunday Worship

bells chime the village awake
singing fills the morning
as congregations gather across the island
bright fabric of Sunday best
accentuates dark skin
smell of roasting pork and taro
pervades the air

but the azure sea patterned dark with reef
calls me loud and low into its heart

here is my church

down among the coral forests
where a myriad of tiny lives
reaffirms how vast creation really is
needing no creator but itself
in infinite selection

in mysteries beyond my ken
I lose myself
floating in a void of wisdom
none can ever know to full extent

in images of fractured light
I catch a glimpse

Myriad

I watched the stars
and learned cold fire burns
sears the mind with images
of vast unending time
where space and distance counterpoint
our finite bounds of earth

I feel the ocean's presence
and revel in the crystalled drop façade
that hides beneath it wonders
immersed in mystery
each convoluted form
an enigma of its own

through forests dark I walk
sensing lives beneath my feet
existences unknown   untouched
no detail spared   unique
miracles in miniature
unnumbered in their grace

step lightly on the earth
so much is still to know

Essence

When Time was born
I wonder did it know what it would see
as aeon after aeon spread their wings
and spiral-danced
across the realm of space?

In agonies of ecstasy
stars ignite
and showered down the elements of life
that fell as stardust through the void.

A quickening became a pulse of love
an essence from that space between the stars
was carried on the solar winds
and given form.

Perfect gravity and atmosphere combined
a fragile, precious mote in time
exquisite chemistries unite
and formed the double helix as the way
the Universe began to know itself.

And Time bears witness to it all
has seen the species rise and fall
each one a note unique
in the music of the spheres.

Expanding ever-outwards
the cosmos rushes on
with galaxies and nebulae in tow
toward that far horizon
where perhaps there is an end
or perhaps a new beginning
as the cycle starts again.

Our dreams are woven in this place
our atoms spun from outer space
we journey on and light the way
like comets in the night
a fleeting blaze of glory
as we grow, evolve and learn of love
and when we need to rest
we'll leave behind our stardust veils
and to those realms return.

Origin

sink through ocean's mirrored sheen
into a world more alien than space
fathoms descend in blue
where first began embodiment of dream
that breathed and tasted form.
In all the history of Time
was this the first   the only?

nature played with shape and size
creation limitless as thought
success and failure tapering the line
a rise and fall of wonderful design.

Heart-trails

A bush track wanders through the heart of me
discovering hidden treasures
and patches of weeds.
Meandering here and there it finds
gems of memory glistening in the dew
of early morning,
conjuring emotions of then.
Side trails run the tangents
of blind alleys
through labyrinthine wastes
of doubt.
But the perfume of spring flowers
pervades.
Enticing, beckoning
the convoluted path unfolds
leading on
to the only destination
that is love.

Lonely Chapel

I The Mourner

Shedding tears in an empty room
stained glass refracts the echoes of the words
rains light upon the lonely pews;
the hollowness within reflects without.
Molten heart struck numb
by wreaths upon the pine.
Where are the ones
whose arms would wrap around?
Far, far away
as whispers on a screen.

II The Mourned

Shedding life in a twilight dream
stained soul refracts in prisms of the light
becoming whole as loneliness departs,
the hollowness now filled within, without.
Overflowing heart
encircles and entwines.
In scattered points of love
I feel them wrap around.
Far-reach
to touch you as I pass.

Note: during the Covid-19 pandemic in 2020, only five mourners were allowed to physically attend a funeral, the rest had to 'attend' via computer.

February Lilies

days after the diagnosis
I had to go away
pulled north by my commitments
the familiar east coast road
became a blur as I drove
numb with shock

only the lilies registered
white lilies by the roadside
all the way to Coffs
and I wondered how the world
would ever be beautiful again
without you in it

the lilies still appear in February
and my throat catches
as I probe that hollow part of me
that aches for you

A Walk in the Wetland

The silkpod vines are seeding in the casuarina forest
silken parachutes cascade on updraughts
delivering hope of future forests.
Cicada song saturates the languid air as surely as the humidity
birds are silent in midday heat
having done their part to usher in the dawn.

Bandicoot and owl curl in secret slumber until dark
beetles hide in folds of melaleuca bark
ants patrol their garrison's expanding territory.
Callistemon is a blur of bee-song
with honey oozing from the crimson tufts.

Light diffuses into shadow-play on forest floor
where a smudge of purple-white
reveals a drift of native violets
and tiny parasols of red and brown
mark mist-damp trails of fungi in the shade.

Time shifts into an illusion
like a walk in faerie land
magic has occurred
and the world within your mind
has changed around you while you walked.

Soundless…

any sound louder than birdsong
is alien in this place
a wrongness done to the forest

the moss absorbs sound
soaks it into the wood of the ancient trees beneath
reservoirs of resonance

time is also captured here
this is a place apart
a moment of peace held in a bubble of green

breath of air from this primordial forest
is an elixir of agelessness

I emerge peaceful
        renewed
                transformed

Gondwana

a thread that shaped
the cut of cloth
weaved its way
through time
contoured the petals
of southern plants
and instigated
maternal pockets
in the beasts

continental drift
has skewed the world
since then

now separate and obtuse
the New World mimics
its Australian kin
and echoes of Gondwanan plants
are bound beneath Antarctic ice

Sea Child

Effervescent   the surf ruffles the shoreline
and clear-lined as shark fins
I sense the furtive life beneath each wave.

Weightless within the spiralling void
I taste a million drops   saltwater wine
pulsing against space and time
the suck and pull of universal tides
echoes deep within my cells.

Porpoise free of surface tension
through aquamarine and turquoise
as   crystalline   the spindrift breath
stays on my skin.

Homage paid
I await again the lunar chant
that percolates saltwater in my veins.

Vocation

Come close in and breathe.
Do you smell the fur and feathers
that are a part of me?

The brindle and the tortoiseshell
pattern me beneath my skin,
a rich tattoo of blended DNA.

The secrets of the species
are mixed into my blood
making vital passage in my veins.

I understand the nuances
of widened eyes
and twitching ears

I speak in fluent feline,
know canine conversations
and dialects of rabbit and of bird.

Intrinsic bonds of trust
where empathy aligns
allows a flow of healing to begin,

and if the journey's end is near
I whisper of the rainbow bridge
and call their angels in.

The glory and the grieving
of the tapestry of life
seeps in through my pores.

Veterinary nurse –
it's not what I do,
it's who I am.

Wreck Dive

Wraiths peripherally appear among skeletal struts
some metamorphose as fish and flashing scales
whilst others vanish, a shimmer of illusion
relics of a former life above the waves.
Steel girders garner life that sham as plants
colours coruscate as tentacles sift brine.

Movement at the edge of light
shadows live as memories resurrect
and voices call the dim companionways
sunken dreams grasping currents
remembered lives a tether to the past
      a siren's song whispers.

Empty cabins, empty hopes
no more to see the sun
the drowned lands of the soul
sleep now in watery dimness
ghosts crowd the empty decks
and haunt the divers' dreams.

The Loch Ard Peacock

How felt the maker
as moulded earthenware
began to shape his dream
exquisite form of throat
proud carriage of the head
with paint and glaze precision
each feather placed
to full effect?

How felt the maker
to be chosen
a badge of the elite
to showcase his wares
for all the world to see
at Melbourne Exposition 1880?
Nine crated, precious birds
were sent to sea.

How felt the maker
upon the news
but one of his creations had survived
had overcome that stretch of deadly reef
and floating there among the dead
      had washed ashore intact
a gilt memorial to fate?

How felt the Maker
to receive
the fifty-two lost souls
the *Loch Ard* had delivered
to the bottom of the sea?

Note: the iron clipper *Loch Ard* was wrecked near Port Campbell,
South Australia, on 1 June 1878 with the loss of fifty-two lives. Two
days after the wreck an intact, life-sized Minton earthenware
peacock was washed ashore in its packing case. The peacock was one
of nine produced and was destined for display at the Melbourne
International Exhibition 1880.

Sea Spirits

Quick as a thought they slide through the ocean
Gliding and diving, delighting in motion.
Twisting and turning back over and under,
Faster than lightning and deeper than thunder.
With a flick of the tail they soar through the sea,
Laughing and loving and living and free.
Riding the bow waves before racing on,
A few precious moments and then – they are gone.
Slipstream of memory caught in a glance
Somersault feelings of joining their dance.

Shearwater

Muttonbird –
a heavy name for a heavy purpose
the evil act lends gravity
to your fragile frame

Shearwater –
the essence of flight
wing tips dipping brine
racing wave tops
seeking the blue

Petrel – St Peter's bird –
dancing on water
air incarnate
heaven – a wingtip away
carving songlines in the sky…

…for the rest of us to follow

ANZAC Storm 2015

as we parade down the Avenue of Allies
we see the green sentinels
      falling, fallen, felled

the enemy was relentless
for days they fought the wind
until they could stand no more

vanquished roots tore trenches
in the sodden earth
and limbs were stretched upon the ground
tasting last breath of life

…like so many of our young men
their blood seeping into the mud
cold limbs stretched on the cold earth
      falling, fallen, felled.

Second-hand War

I was a child when that war waged
no fears of death eclipsed my world
Vietnam was a word I heard on TV news
       and paid no mind
but I grew up and fell in love
with a man who buried scars
behind the brash and easy smiles he kept as walls.

Scant memories you've shared with me
       no man should hold in mind
       God help the ones you do not share
my soul aches for your pain
and I bleed as do you
on each ANZAC Day's reminder.

Those memories will not heal
       those faces did not vanish with homecoming
and they who spat upon your return
could not know the seeds of pain they sowed
that would blossom when the tide of time was full
and the anger overflowed
       in drowned sorrows in a bottle.

I would tame your nightmares if I could
I would erase your mind's eye sight
       of bleeding terrors in the jungle
       and children strung on fences
and mates gone mad with the grief of it.

I was only a child when that war waged
second-hand, I have become
a victim of its hate
tethered to its legacy
      by a band of gold.

My Nightmare

Today I chose to breakfast in the pergola
the garden's stillness called me through the fog
too early for other motel guests
I sat alone in the chill
remembering past holiday nights
of closeness and passion.

So sad we now must sleep in separate beds
limiting the nightly struggle
of restlessness and harm.
I try not to resent
the nightmares of your past
that distance you from me.

Adrift

Back to the womb I go
Find peace in the arms of the ocean
Rocked in the cradle of life
And gentled by its motion.

The surge and tug of the tide
Lifts the demons from my soul
Bears me up on its salty swell
Delivers me hale and whole.

Whenever sorrows gather
And I can't get to the sea
I close my eyes and taste the brine
And find the sea in me.

Sunset Song

Sit with me at sunset
where ripples spread
on the burnished copper surface
of the bay
when the mullet jump.

Here at close of day
breathe in stillness
as wild swans
fly low across calm waters.

Sit with me at sunset
and listen
as the story of this bay
whispers its song.

Tonight the full moon
calls the waters,
our closest kin
who bore witness
when fiery breath
of earth first birthed this place

watched as rainforests
clothed the coast
and then receded
as drier times held sway

saw the tribes move in
to settle by the river
only to be swept apart
by a rising sea
as ice caps melted at the poles.

And so, this bay was born.

The ever-present constancy
of change
becomes the rhythm,
the melody of life
is woven through our days.

Sit with me at sunset
and sing with me
the ancient song of this land.
Your heart has ears –
it knows the tune.

The Time Box

a little box of time
has come into my hands
wrapped in ribbons
from the future

in rainbow dreams and whispers
I hear the echoes of tomorrow
calling
tantalising
filaments of the web
are touched and change
direction of the flow
perhaps before its time

life is made from
elements of now

a glimpse ahead to when?
do I dare look?
what would that knowing do?

if good
I might just wish away today
never live
if bad
fall into dark despondency
lose hope

Pandora had a box like this
        think I'll leave it on the shelf

Stars of Earth

Autumn leaves like frozen fireworks
no less brilliant for their stillness
static stars in gold   magenta
mark the boughs as maple leaves
crimson cascades of claret ash
rival tangerines and reds of rhus
poplar   ornamental peach
are rioting yellow
as April moves to May

the chill of June brings change
one by one the leaves detach
comet colours fading with the days
amber-hued they fall to star the earth

Just Add Water

Take the track at the end of that street, you know the one, where the sign says 'Do Not Enter', the one we all use all the time.

Go around the sandy bit where troubled adolescent souls go to vent their frustration with society on the wrecks of stolen cars.

Look   down   NOW.

Open your eyes to the visions, your ears to the music, your heart to the magic.

No plans, just follow your feet. I hope you didn't wear your watch – this place is *timeless.*

And just   like   that your breathing slows to the pace of what surrounds you and the wonder fills in the blanks.

See the tiny velvet mite, no bigger than a pinhead, going about its business on the bark. Dragonflies hover above the ferns. A black and orange butterfly leads you on, down another trail.

It has rained. The ants have fortified their walls against the deluge, building a moat around their entranceway. Higher and higher, how much rain did they expect? The ground is damp and that allows the mystery of autumn to ignite.

In a myriad of forms they come, silently pushing up through the earth to show their secrets to the world, to those who care to see. They have waited for the rain.

All year they do their work under the earth, sharing their song with the trees in a harmony of life. 'Red and yellow and pink and green, purple and orange and blue.' They sing a rainbow to the world and make it work.

From the sandy-loam blind caps emerge, opening gill parasols ripe with spores to spread their love through the forest. Cascades of tiny, filamentous fungi, fluted cups, turreted corals, creamy veils, painted velvets, fairy gardens of puffballs, stars and jellied fruits.

They are the gift that comes with autumn rains. Let the carnival begin.

Interwoven

Somewhere in the silence
Are the answers that I seek
Perhaps beside a waterfall
Or by a flowing creek.

Somewhere in the silence
Is the sum of all that's known
In the patience of the mountains
And the forests that have grown.

Somewhere in the silence
There are ways to find the key
Among the sparkling droplets
On the shores of every sea.

Somewhere in the silence
In the chronicles of time
Lies the music of the planets
Pulsing rhythm, breathing rhyme.

Somewhere in the silence
Only whispered words can tell
Are the secrets of a lifetime
Bedded down in every cell.

Immersed

Through sunlit shafts and turquoise blue
sapphire deeps and coral trenches
with salty tears I find my way
      here   where the great whales move with grace
turning and gliding with twitch of tail   flick of fin
      here   in the fluid void
effortlessly they pirouette
changing partners and sinking deep
while their whispers echo with the tides
voicing dimensions of time and space
singing the stars and moon and sun
birthing universes within me with their presence

the vibrations of their being
unravel the pathways of my life
      like shedding skin
all my days have led to now
and I have been changed

for I have danced in the sea with giants
found absolution beneath the waves
and risen from the depths reborn.

Serenade

beneath the waves
our descent is bathed in song

alien notes
    surround
    caress

a tunnel of sound
heard and felt to the core
    timeless
    nameless

wisdom etched in every note
from when the universe was born
    enigmatic
    profound

angels of Light
singing the mysteries
    of Life
    of Love
    of Being

the sound goes on forever
    and takes us with it

Sea

the sea breathes me in
claims me as one of its own
and the misunderstood mermaid
comes home

with liquid strokes
the coral reef caresses
vibrant life seethes
their colours explore my senses

diamond shimmer on the surface
sinks into my bones
magical elixir of sunlight and salt
ambrosia on my tongue

passing whales sing me awake
lead me deep
to become one
with the heart
      and pulse
           of the ocean

Hawkesbury

Glaciers gouged this river valley
the grinding stones of the moraine displacing earth
until the planet warmed and melted ice.

Now mangroves line the shores
Far-reach till brine dilutes to fresh
bind silt to manufacture islands.

Pale globes of jellyfish
ghost up from the depths
to feast on sunlight.

Split sandstone colours
like a captured sunset
lie revealed at water's edge

where wading birds
revel in mud
overseen by watching eagle eyes.

Cicadas saturate summer air with song
hypnotise senses with their drone
but symbolise the nature of this place.

In rocky grottoes fig trees spread
their ancient canopies
a sanctuary from the heat.

The river flows drown sound
eclipse time
the spirit of the *Deerubin*
lives on.

* *Deerubin* is the local Aboriginal word for the Hawkesbury River, Dharug Country.

Wild Places

Tasmania

All the world was once like this
Rampant   awesome
gorges filled with fern trees
ancient pines   towering gums
beeches old beyond knowing
wildness raw and verdant
crashing down in cascades of forest, rock and stream.

> Forests crowd river banks to water's height
> pushing outwards   reaching
> overtaking the ruins of man's ventures
> as if they'd never been.
> Tumbled boulders, moss and ferns channel wild waters
> crystal droplets pour their souls beyond the brink
> as falling thunder
> creating air as pure as first primeval breath.

> > Limitless beach   an edge between the worlds
> > rolling swell that has not tasted land
> > for endless miles
> > birthing waves upon the western shores
> > to tumble stones an aeon offered up from under ice.

> > > Untamed   untrodden   unmarked by man
> > > life so 'alive' it overwhelms the senses
> > > pure nature undiluted.
> > > Behind my eyes and in my heart
> > > I take it home.

Top End

Escape from southern winter state
Where the sea is always east
Into the land of the Gagudju
Wetland plains and jabiru
And the country of the beast.

Blue waters beckon in the heat
Sun shimmers on the sea
But swimming here is not advised
For one who lurks with watchful eyes
Would make a meal of me.

Yet in such danger beauty lies
The silent hunter stalks the sands
Precise and elegant and bold
Delivered from its primal mould
The king surveys his lands.

A million waterbirds abound
By monsoon lake and lily pools
Magpie goose and pelican
But 40,000 years of man
And the crocodile still rules.

Beyond The Wall

The Resort

a tiny slice of home
set in this gem of the Pacific
three meals a day
a vast array of food and fun
activities from dawn to dusk
familiar to our lives
with small offerings of island life
       pasteurised
to satisfy our curiosity

beyond the wall
a different world silently exists
no sparkling streetlights here
or spacious rooms with en suites
no refrigerators full of food
just hand-me-down clothes
school for only those who can afford it
meagre meals and fewer prospects

yet look again
full church on Sunday mornings
kids play outside in fresh air
with makeshift toys and   laughing
fresh food picked daily from the village garden
meals lovingly made by those with time to cook
family ties unbroken through the generations

and ask yourself
dear tourist
with funds to fly around the world
who is the poorer?

Tea Towels

switch down a gear
go into autopilot
no need to think
just do

suds and sponge
dip and rinse
rack and dry

reach for the tea towel
patterns catch your eye
where did you buy it?
a souvenir of some past trip

and suddenly you're lazing
on that sunny beach in Queensland
taking coral baths with languorous fish

sand so white
sun so warm
a million miles away from this sink!

damn!
The washing up is finished
back to reality.

Bird Language

A hundred voices fill the air at dawn
waking the world
colouring the layers of the soundscape
from a palette of blended tones.

Songs will anchor this day
for those with ears to hear
a subtle language of the sky
a hundred songs with a thousand meanings.
From tiny throats the story of the world unfolds
truth-saying the minutes that pass
rhythming the hours.
The cadences will rise and fall
with the telling.
A new story every day
from a theme as old as time.

Strangest Fruit

from the branches
plump globes hang
dark and pungent
tough skin wraps
tender flesh

come nightfall
skins unfurl to wings
fly forth
to harvest forest bounty

No Trace

no bones lie hidden deep in buried shale
no tar pit excavations have revealed
no spoor of herds in sediments of river bed
no remnants fallen in a limestone cave
no family tree of equine origin is traced
no skeletal pedigree with one-horned signature
has ever been unearthed

elusive beast
though somehow more believable
than Tyrannosaurus rex
of which there is no doubt
you persist
where solid proof would make less real the dream

and who's to say
upon some parallel plane
your herds do not graze peacefully in verdant meadows?
is fantasy the door through which your ghost slips in
to bring magic to our world?

The Voice in the Sea

The voice in the sea
whispers…
the song of the sand
in the reeds on the dunes
in the evening.

The voice in the sea
whispers…
the roar and the hiss
as the waves beat out time
on the beaches.

The voice in the sea
whispers…
the crash and the sigh
of the ebb and the flow
in the rock pools.

The voice in the sea
whispers…
in ethereal tones
as the final great whales
echo deeply.

The solemn waters
tell their tale
to those who listen with inner ears
who feel with their soul
and follow their heart's quiet wisdom.

Will the world stop to hear
the water's plea?
Do you listen
to the voice in the sea
as it whispers…?

Extinction

I am silent tonight as I lie here alone
The short autumn days bring a chill to my bones
So I dig down for warmth, buy a little more time
With the knowledge within – I'm the last of my kind.

Once we were abundant and covered this land
In crevice and burrow 'neath red desert sand.
The nights we would play under round desert moons
We hunted and loved to our own rhythmic tunes.

A part of the song that nature had weaved
Enriching the earth, from the seed to the leaves
Intricate part of mysterious web
Each species entranced by a dance that was led.

What now of the mulga that we helped grow strong?
What now of the parrots who shared in our song?
A hole will be left in the pattern of life
Oh, how will the weft and the warp mend this strife?

My passing, unnoticed by most of the world,
Sends ripples and ripples that roll and unfurl
And down through the ages the angels will weep
As I ready myself for that eternal sleep.

Unique in the world, and yet now never more
So turn out the light, close that final door.
And a voice in my heart says there never will be
A creature evolving exactly like me.

Sorrow

a sea of sorrow
deeper than grief
has swallowed my heart
and laps at my soul

the desecrated landscapes
lie barren to the core
and no amount of time
will heal the wounds complete

the screaming air
the nightmare sky
all future hope
has vanished in the smoke

it has begun
the world is burning now
but from the ashes
what will rise?

change will come
and from the fringes
life will seep back in
but never the same
the originals are forever ceased

three billion little lives as ash
unique and perfect strands of DNA
gone
genetic lines
broken
potential generations
lost
spirals of the double helix
burned into oblivion
three billion souls
as fodder for the flames

in the hollow of me
I feel them still

Cycles

stark grey fingers claw the air
beseeching sky
in parody of prayer to gods who pay no heed

the earth becomes mosaic art
cracks stretching wide between clods
hillside forests perish on the slopes
dry wells encountered by their seeking roots

wedge-tail lifts on thermals over hills
seeking life but finding death
it feeds around the ruts of clay
that once were dams

storm clouds circle on the winds
and blessed rain at last begins to fall

mosaic cracks become a channel to the creek
ducks bookmark the river with a 'V'
and verdancy returns to bank and vale

barren paddocks farm the sun again
new grass turning light into life
where patient cows lift weary heads to graze
and remnant flocks survey a transformed world

a patch of sky has fallen to the field
and made a blue oasis of the mud

Becoming

perhaps it was the quality of light through rain
that made the new bark seem to incandesce
shedding their old skin the grey gums glowed
like candles through the forest

cicadas serenaded summer heat
singing their joy of release
from restraints of the growing years
the dream of flight now realised and true

through change
the world
our lives
progress

onward and flowing through the change
shedding layers of ourselves
with every twist and turn of life
our loves   our griefs   our aspirations
all pass from one to the next
we become more than we were before
and each moment becomes our world

looking up   in circles in the sky   I see the wedge-tails
and know that today I am blessed by eagles

Sacred Exchange

As I breathe out
the trees breathe in
a trail of molecules
leads backwards to an ancient sea
to where it all began.

Through time the symbiosis
has entwined us all
with pulse of sap
and beat of heart
the circle is complete
and we may walk as one
and never be alone.

August Rising

The insects are rising with the season
from dormant states
or newly hatched
a steady stream of life
emerges from the green

a thousand ants have gathered
on the bricks
as royalty with wings
depart the nest
with mission to deploy genetic codes
to farther fields

undone suits of spiders
ornament the webs
mimic life as breezes
twist and turn
while further down the sill
their older, larger selves
display new coats.

there's buzzing in the air
as wasps construct their nests
from paper parasols
and muddy tubes
to honeycombs
and holes in ground or wood
another generation
starts to grow

the birds and bats will feast
another cycle of the year
has just begun.

Tanilba

The name means 'place of white flowers'
in ancient dialect
and every spring the land is filled
with petals, flannel-soft

the dawning wakes to eerie cries
and sea mist drifting in from the bay

languid wing-flaps carry the callers
to the high tree tops
to breakfast on pine and casuarina cones
huge beaks tearing at the wood

yellow tails and cheeks against black feathers
link past to present
remind of ochre on dark skin
this is the land of the Worimi

follow in their footsteps
along the sandy tracks of Wallum heath
to where froglets call from the reed beds
and paperbarks dip their toes in wetland pools

sunset skies through mangrove fringe
reflect in water held in rocks
sculpted from earth's molten heart
millennia ago

midnight stars brush angophora branches
and the night is as hushed as owl wings.

Rainbow Refuge

I close my eyes
and instantly the breeze
has carried me to where
black cockatoos call
high, high in the pines

images of lorikeets
rainbowing the bottlebrush
with blue and orange
as pink galahs plunder seed heads
from the paddock grasses

bowerbirds green and satin blue
pluck blackberries
beyond the fenceline
and once
a flash of regent gold

the ever-changing valley
misty in the autumn morning
shining silver with the overflow
of flooded creek or
lush and verdant
under summer sun

veranda cool and welcoming
comfortable as a mother's hug
where night time skies
beckon with a million stars
a haven for the heart

Dispersal

My mother's wind chimes
accent the breeze with music
and I am back in the broad-verandaed house
overlooking paddocks that are there no more

the small, neat unit
surrounded by the swirl of traffic noise
is now their home
but they will never   truly
reside here

carried on those melodic notes
the chimes journey me through time
to a place of serenity
forever kept in a corner of my mind –
my mother with her cup of tea
the emerald pasture, silver creek
cats purring on the old wood floor

memories are captured in moments
held in safe-keeping by the senses
to be dispensed at later times
when sparked to life
by the movement of the wind
a scent of fresh-mown lawn
the lift of a butterfly's wings

transported to another place in time
in that instant
to be again that part of you
that lives eternally within
until displaced by the intrusion of now

when she passed on
my mother's things
were dispersed among her family and friends

a visit here today
has taken me back
as she lives on
within the hearts and minds
of those she loved

Haiku

Patonga

the sea never sleeps
but pauses in quiet bays
to catch its breath

Corona

Do you feel the shift?
Listen to the wind of change
sculpting the future.

Quest

The Fibonacci patterns beckon
and down the rabbit hole I go,
falling like Alice
witnessing impossibilities
of spiralling galaxies
        dinosaur bones
                the eyestalks of snails.

Mysteries beyond magic
unlock secret doors
to intricate dimensions
wonder finding a voice
        in the infinite
answers that lead
        to questions unfathomable.

Devouring everything the caterpillar has to offer,
through the looking glass we go
leaving behind the residue
of stone age huts
        and rocket ships
                of who we were before.

Note: Fibonacci numbers are of interest to biologists and physicists because they are frequently observed in various natural objects and phenomena. The branching patterns in trees and leaves, for example, and the distribution of seeds in a raspberry are based on Fibonacci numbers.

Earthed

I put my hands into the soil
and the world skews sideways
my cyber-brain of
      emails
              facebook
                      websites
slowly drizzles through my fingers
to bind with the sandy grains
in the reality of now

I feel myself solid
as roots go down
from the headspace void

here there is only dirt

the sparking mental arc
has finally been
      earthed.

About the Author

Since the age of ten, Jeannie Lawson has dedicated her life to fighting for the environment, being the recipient over the ensuing fifty years of several state and national awards for her volunteer work. Nature, particularly that of the oceans, has been her passion and her refuge, her work and her spiritual touchstone. She feels deeply about the world, the people in it and the things that happen to them and this collection of poems reflects all of this. Although Jeannie has had many of her poems published over the years, this is the first collection of her own works, with another in the pipeline. She resides in Port Stephens in NSW, where she works in environmental education through whale watching, NPWS and in her own business – Harmony Visions Eco-Tours.

www.ingramcontent.com/pod-product-compliance
Lightning Source LLC
Chambersburg PA
CBHW071034080526
44587CB00015B/2609